We gratefully acknowledge the financial support of the Government of Canada through the Book Publishing Industry Development Program (BPIDP) for our publishing activities.

 Conseil des Arts   Canada Council
du Canada   for the Arts

Publisher: Jennifer Canham
Associate Publisher: Angela Keenlyside
Editorial Director: Mary Beth Leatherdale
Creative Director: Barb Kelly
Design Coordinator: Susan Sinclair
Editor: John Crossingham
Production Coordinator: Paul Markowski
Production Editor: Larissa Byj
Production Assistant: Kathy Ko

Designer: Clayton Hanmer

Thanks to Craig Battle, Mandy Ng, OWL Think Tank, Jeff Szpirglas and the Grade 6 students at Ventura Park Public School.

Library and Archives Canada Cataloguing in Publication

Hanmer, Clayton, 1978-
     CTON's super a-maze-ing year of crazy comics : puzzles, mazes, blobs and more / Clayton Hanmer.

Collection of comics, mazes, puzzles, etc. from OWL magazine.
ISBN 978-2-89579-209-3

     I. Title.   II. Title: CTON's super a-maze-ing year of crazy comics.
III. Title: OWL magazine.

PN6733.H35 2008   j741.5'971   C2008-903258-6

This book is dedicated to Clay, my parents, and our family for putting up with all my craziness. —CTON

Printed and bound in Canada

Owlkids Publishing
10 Lower Spadina Ave., Suite 400
Toronto, ON M5V 2Z2
Ph: 416.340.2700
Fax: 416.340.9769

Publisher of

chirp   chickaDEE   OWL
www.owlkids.com

HEYA!

Welcome to my crazy comic book!!! It's super silly and full of all sorts of wicked, fun stuff like mazes, comics about my pal Blob, cool forts, and even how to plant a tree! Pretty cool, huh?! So grab yourself a nice big chair and get all comfy with us!

CTON
(say see-ton)

Yep, me Blob!

CTON'S SUPER A-MAZE-ING YEAR OF CRAZY COMICS!

TABLE of CONTENTS

MORE CHEEZ!

HOME OF CTON & FRIENDS: ~ WWW.CTON.CA ~ DROP ON BY AND SAY HI! CTON

DING DONG

THE BIRTH OF BLOB

LOOK! This show you how draw me, Blob!

① Draw outline.

good one →

② Put eyes in.

me eyes → ∎ ∎

③ Now add mouth.

nice teeths →

④ More stuff.
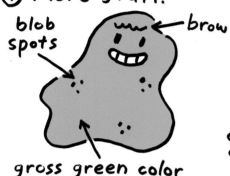
blob spots
brow
gross green color

⑤ Need slime puddle!

yuck! →

⑥ Done!

GOOD JOB! Me so handsome!

Me also show you how draw Blab, me hillbilly cousin! Cool!!!

① Draw outline.

you know how →

② Eyes next with cutesy eye lashes.

she a girl →

③ Don't forget mouth!

fake teeth (ha ha) →

④ Add hillbilly stuff.

pigtails (orange)
straw hat (hee haw!)
dirty blob spots

⑤ Blab also have slime!

Nasty! →

⑥ All done, pardner!

Yippee-Ki-yay!

BLOB & BLAB'S
FALL FASHIONS

squash (Blab's fave veggie)

straw hat for fall hoedowns

Blab

Blob's country cousin

toasted pumpkin seeds for later

back-to-school stuff

bag of berries defrosting to make a pie

MATH

a squirrel stuck trying to hide its winter acorns

fall-themed slime that is even better than Blob's...

Blob-style jack-o-lantern

BLOB's HARVEST HOEDOWN!!!

Help Blob match up Farmer Bill's farm animals with their weird, yet proper, names!

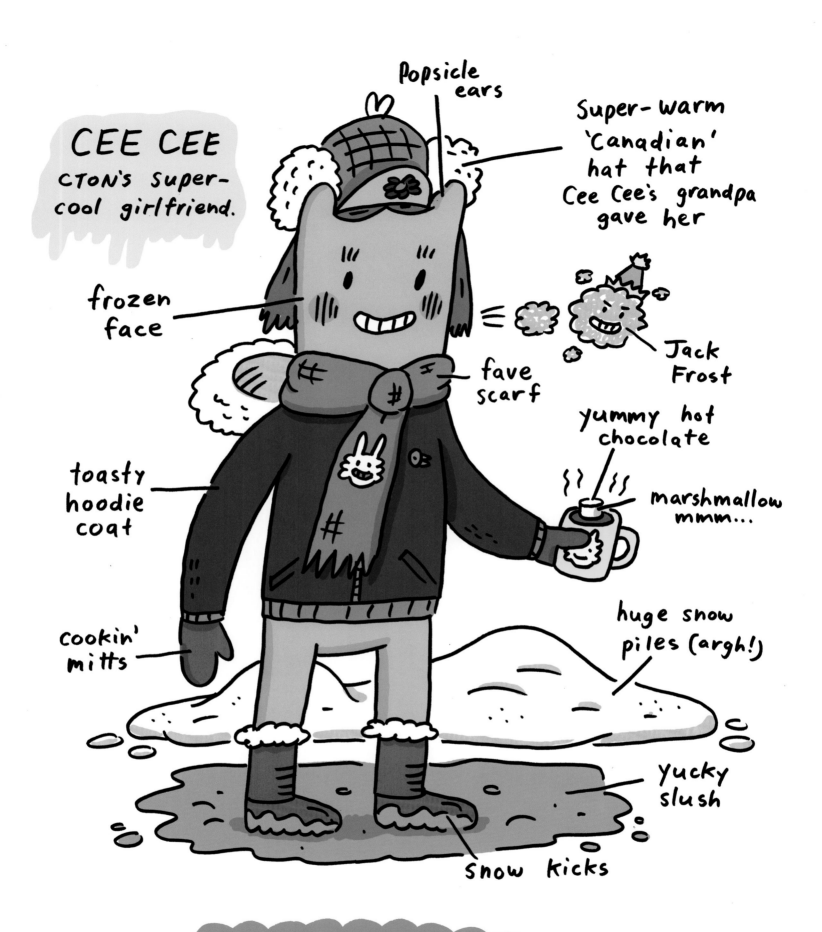

Hot chocolate contains special minerals that allow you to withstand the winter air.

The largest recorded snowman was so huge that he didn't melt for thirteen years!

Polar bear fur isn't white. They have it dyed to match the snow because they are very fashion conscious.

There are worms that live in ice. Known as Bubba Ice Worms, they call mountain glaciers home and wear funny little hats.

WEIRD WINTER MYTHS!!

Santa prefers to use female reindeer because male reindeer always either forget their antlers or smell really, really bad.

I'm outta here...

Reindeer survive the Arctic winter by building secret underground fortresses with large fireplaces, huge-screen TV's, hot tubs, and buckets of hot chocolate.

SECRET FORTRESS ↓

OH NO! Good thing I brought this here beaver tail...

In winter, beavers live off fat stored in their tails while buried deep inside their beaver lodges. They also keep cinnamon and chocolate sauce on hand to make their beaver tails taste awesome!

chocolate

ZZZZ

Snowflakes come from outer space and contain miniature beings who are on a vacation to Earth. The largest snowflake found was as large as a car and tasted like rainbow sherbet.

27

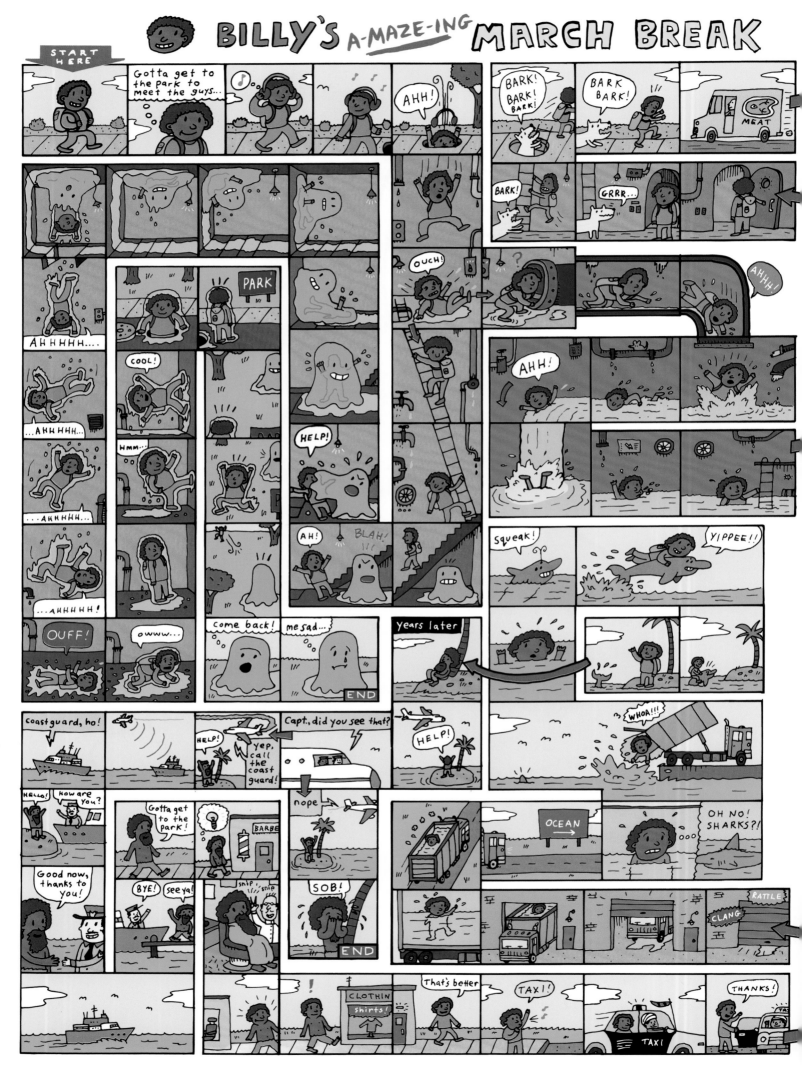

ADVENTURE

Help Billy find his way to the park to hang out with his friends.

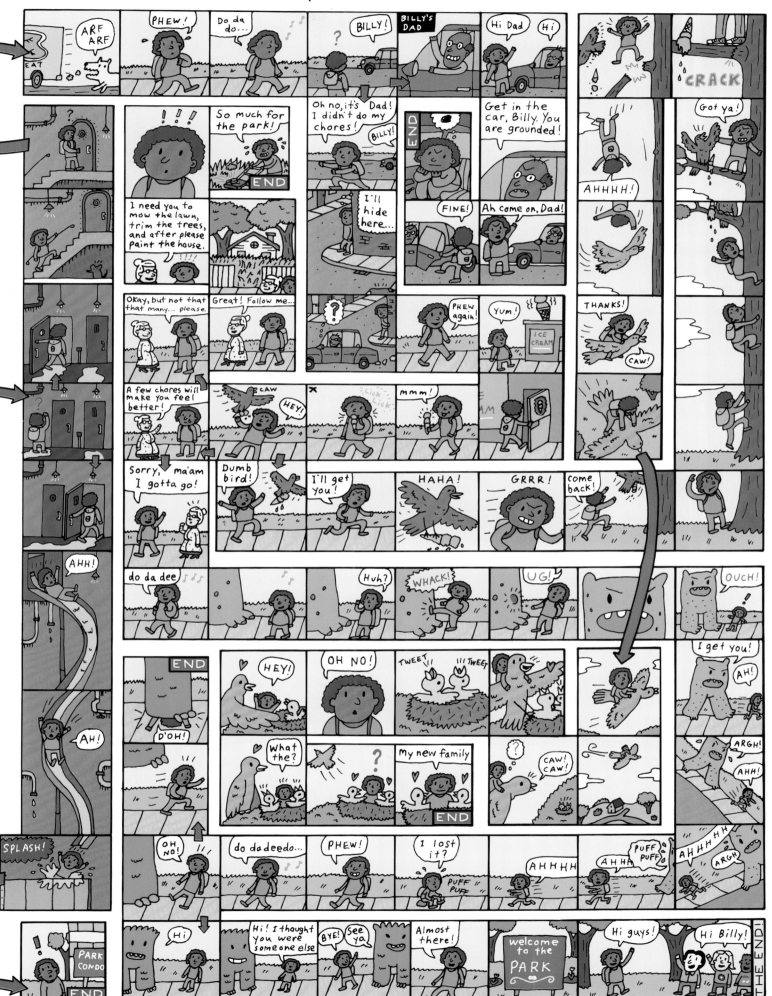

BLOB STRIKES BACK!

Oops! Blob dropped his comic strip on the way to the printer. Study the panels to help him put it back in order!

BILLY & SUZIE'S
SPRING STYLES

Let's Plant a Tree!

CToN shows you how to plant a tree in your own backyard. *

Things you'll need:

Shovel

bucket of water

tree food (fertilizer)*

nice little tree

① First, dig a hole big enough for the tree's roots in a nice open spot on the lawn.*

*Ask your parents first!

② Next pour a little water and tree food into the hole.

③ Remove the root bag and place tree into the hole.

bag

④ While a helper holds the tree upright, fill the hole with dirt.

STAMP!

STOMP!

⑤ Now stomp down the dirt around the tree so it stands up straight and on its own.

⑥ Finally, pour some more water and tree food at the base of your newly planted tree friend.

⑦ TA-DAH! A new tree buddy has a home in your yard!

Watch your new pal grow and help make the air we breathe nice and clean for everyone! Thanks, tree!

clean air

WICKED!

CTON & CEE CEE'S
SUMMER STITCHES

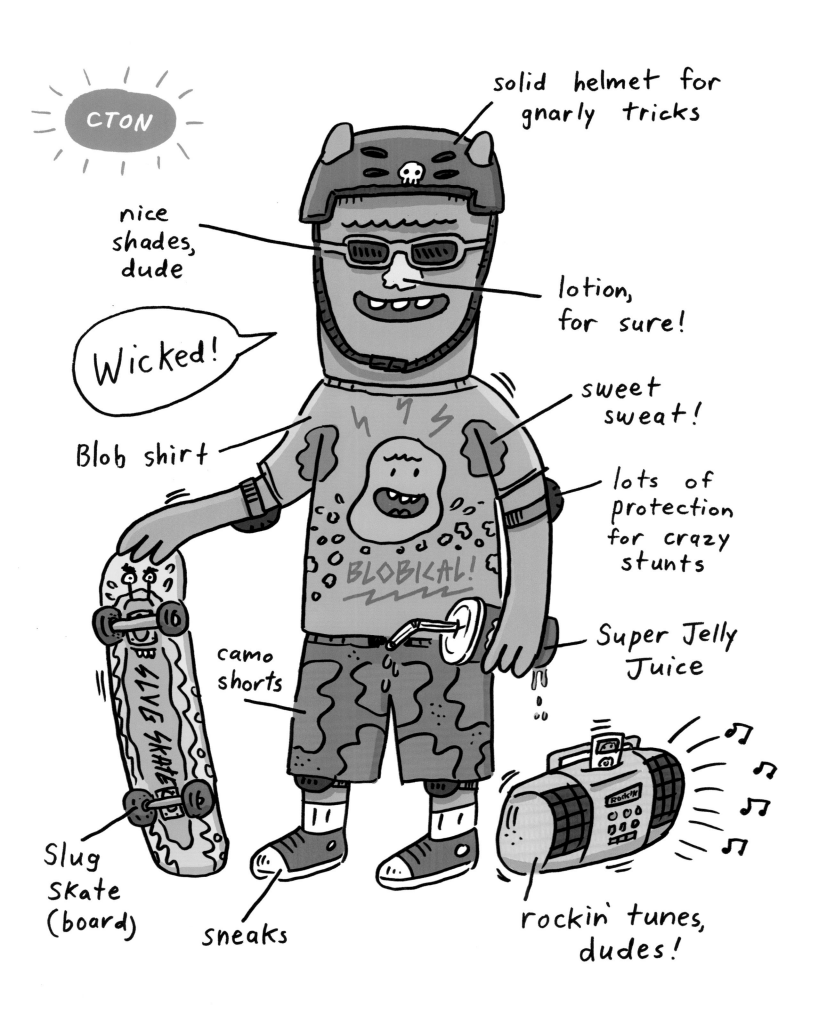

CTON's CRAZY COMIC TIPS!

How to build a comic strip.

solid frames

creative shapes

Over this way, Bill!

organization of your story

Hi there

Hi

What kind of bear are you?

bright colors

A hungry one!

witty characters

Creating intelligence in any situation.

①
stupid pear

②
add glasses

③
add buckteeth and freckles

Three steps to a buff character.

① heya!

② mmph!

③ oh yeah!

I ♥ comics

How to make anything into a unicorn.

① regular old tissue box

② magical horn — stars — wings

ta-dah! a unicorn!

Three ways to use a cloud.

whistles

mad cows

little old ladies

When in doubt, add a moustache!

① boring!

② much better!

How to class up your comic characters.

before

after

Adding personality to your characters.

unibrow — wig — glasses — crazy teeth — scar — beard

53

SO?

What did you think of all that rad stuff? Did you master drawing Blob or make a cool pillow fort of your own? Sorry to break the news, but this book is done! Don't worry, though, because Blob and I are always ready for a new and wacky adventure... especially in our next super-crazy book! Until then, check out www.cton.ca, and make sure to keep on drawing!

your pal, CTON

Comics rule!

Before we go, here are the ANSWERS to all the mazes and puzzles in the book!

p. 8

p. 14

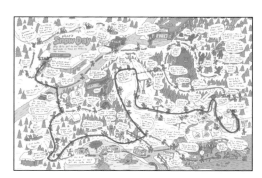

p. 20

I hope you cleaned up your slime after that farm visit, Blob!

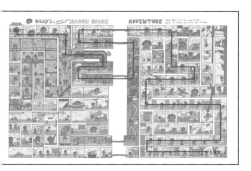

p. 32

p. 34

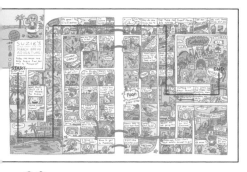

p. 38

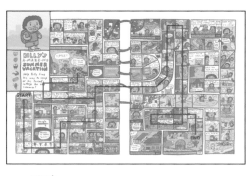

p. 44

Mmm... Sushi!